LOVE

HEARTFELT QUOTES

More books by Claire Bruce

Coming Soon

Joy

Friendship

LOVE

HEARTFELT QUOTES

by

C L A I R E B R U C E

SABI SUNDAY PRESS

PLEASANT PRAIRIE, WI

LOVE: HEARTFELT QUOTES

Copyright © 2022 by Claire Bruce

Published by Sabi Sunday Press
Pleasant Prairie, WI

Design by Belle & Lauren, LLC

This book is available for special discounts for bulk purchases for sales, promotions, or premiums. For more information, contact the publisher at www.sabisundaypress.com

ISBN 979-8-9870643-0-6

Printed in the USA

To those we love

and who inspire love.

CONTENTS

Introduction

9

Quotations

Ending Thoughts

53

Sources

54

love   pag-ibig   amare   salang
aahkyit   liefde   kärlek   milovat
kærlighed   rakkaus   aimer   liebe
pyaar   updendo   soyayya   aloha
grá   armastus   ást   hak   szeretet
jacayl   asanninneq   cinta   laska
uthando   hlub   aroha   mohabbat
libe   evin   imħabba   yêu   meilė
alofa   prēma   miłość   ai   anpu
pi'āra   dragoste   khair   lyubov
gaol   tresna   dashuri   adaraya
sneha   ài   maitri   sevgi   cariad
agapi   maitasuna   rąk   hobb   aşk
renmen   ljubav   amore   mīlestība

*L*ove. For many, the word may initially conjure hues and nuances of pinks and deep reds, romance, and a haze of sweet emotions. We know, however, that there is a great variety of love that encompasses even greater levels of intensity and complexity.

Love is grand, but it doesn't always have to be "grand". It is a mighty emotion that can be expressed, felt, and enjoyed on a more mundane level and in the simplest of ways. I am sure it's the everyday and simple expressions of love that help see many of us through our day. That is the beauty of love.

Love will transform those who are in its thrall or consumed by it. On one end, it can push a person to greater and triumphant heights; on the other, to the deep depths of despair.

In its most noble state, a spirit of generosity, gratitude, understanding, and true forgiveness will always prevail.

At its happiest and most poetic, a sweet bouquet arises, surrounding us with a fragrance that will encapsulate one's entire being until it simply flows over and must be expressed.

Sadly, through the loss of love or a loved one, we experience hurt, profound sadness, even anger, and regret. We may even question our faith. Where love is concerned, we cannot be indifferent.

Love is the fiber that strengthens our will and allows us to do things we normally wouldn't have or accomplish things in an inspired or graceful manner. It keeps us hopeful, excitedly waiting in anticipation of things to come: a dream, a desire, or a promise to be fulfilled.

Love is a powerful force to be reckoned with, to befriend, and cultivate. In its right environment, it gives birth to its own; its contagiousness spreads. Love has to be shared. It has to be given away.

Love is abstract; it comes and goes. It exists without words but shows its true self and manifests itself in various acts and deeds, for only then could its power be seen and felt.

In truth, the smallest or greatest of deeds, when done or received with love, creates the same powerful impact. It leaves us in a much better state than before; a magical transformation where both giver and recipient are never the same.

This book is but a small collection of quotations about love that spans the ages. Its focus is primarily on what is love, romantic love, and love for oneself and mankind. When putting this together, I'm reminded of an instructor who once said that when reading short phrases or sentences, pause and let it sink in for just a moment. What do you think it means? How does it make you feel?

With some of these quotes, I felt the emotion right away; some I had to stop and think a bit. Whether it's someone's perception of what is love, a romantic love found, lost, or unrequited, I'll hope you'll find meaning, something stirring, and maybe a little humor inside.

Powerful and mighty. That is love.

Claire Bruce

" *Love* is patient, love is kind.
It does not envy, it does not boast,
it is not proud."

- 1 Corinthians 13:4

"Love conquers all things; let us, too,
give in to love."
- Virgil

"Love does not dominate; it cultivates."
- Johann Wolfgang von Goethe

"One word frees us of all the weight and pain
of life. That word is love."
- Sophocles

"Life is the flower for which love is the honey."
- Victor Hugo

"Love, love, love, that is the soul of genius."
- Wolfgang Amadeus Mozart

"The purest expression of love is an outflow
from a heart that overflows."
- Mary Ann Baylon

"Love is the whole thing. We are only pieces."
- Rumi

"It makes no difference as to the name of the god
since love is the real God of all the world."
- Apache Proverb

"Where there is love, there is life."
- Mahatma Gandhi

"Love is trembling happiness."
- Khalil Gibran

"Love is the most beautiful thing to have,
the hardest thing to earn, and the most
painful thing to lose."
- Unknown

"Love does not claim possession but
gives freedom."
- Rabindranath Tagore

"How do you spell 'love'?" - Piglet
"You don't spell it…you feel it." – Pooh
- A. A. Milne

"Love recognizes no barriers. It jumps hurdles,
leaps fences, penetrates walls to arrive at
its destination full of hope."
- Maya Angelou

"Love, like death, the universal leveler
of mankind."

- William Congreve

"Kindness eases change, love quiets fear."

- Octavia Butler

"You cannot touch love either, but you can feel the
sweetness that it pours into everything."

- Helen Keller

"Love is the greatest refreshment in life."

- Pablo Picasso

"Love is the desire to give, not to
receive something."

- Bertolt Brecht

"Life! What art thou without love?"
- E. Moore

"Love never claims, it ever gives.
Love ever suffers, never resents, never
revenges itself."
- Mahatma Gandhi

"Love is the emblem of eternity; it confounds
all notion of time; effaces all memory of a
beginning, all fear of an end."
- Madame de Stael

"Many waters cannot quench love, neither can
the floods drown it."
- Song of Solomon

"Love is of all passions the strongest,
for it attacks simultaneously the head,
the heart, and the senses."

- Lao Tzu

"A life lived in love will never be dull."

- Leo Buscaglia

"Love is the absence of judgment."

- Dalai Lama

"Love is the only force capable of transforming
an enemy into a friend."

- Martin Luther King, Jr.

"Real love, no matter how unworthy the object, is a glorious adventure. It bursts the shackles of selfishness. One's world is bigger, broader; one's sympathies are amazingly more tender. No matter what the result, if you haven't really loved, you haven't really lived."

- Emilie Loring

"Love is an irresistible desire to be
irresistibly desired."
- Robert Frost

"Drink to me only with thine eyes,
and I will pledge with mine;
or leave a kiss but in the cup
and I'll not look for wine."
- Ben Johnson

"I am grateful that you were born, and that
your love is mine, and our two lives woven
and welded together!"
- Mark Twain

"Love is composed of a single soul
inhabiting two bodies."
- Aristotle

"In one kiss, you'll know all I haven't said."
- Pablo Neruda

"If I know what love is, it is because of you."
- Herman Hesse

"Fate has us meet from a thousand miles away."
- Chinese Proverb

"Love makes your soul crawl from its
hiding place."
- Zora Neal Hurston

"My waking thoughts are all of thee."
- Napoleon Bonaparte

"You are my heart, my life, my one
and only thought."
- Sir Arthur Conan Doyle

"She walks in beauty, like the night
Of cloudless climes and starry skies;
And all that's best of dark and bright
Meet in her aspect and her eyes…"
- Lord Byron

"Romance is the glamour that changes the dust
of everyday life into a golden haze."
- Elinor Glynn

"I know no other reason to love
than to love you."
- Fernando Pessoa

"One day, you will ask me which is
more important: my life or yours. I will say
mine and you will walk away not knowing
that you are my life."
- Khalil Gibran

"On a night when the moon shines brightly
as this, the unspoken thoughts of even the most
discreet heart might be seen."
- Izumi Shikibu

"I wish you to know that you have been
the last dream of my soul."
- Charles Dickens

"The sweetest of all sounds is that
of the voice of the woman we love."
- Jean de La Bruyère

"Each day I love you more; today more than
yesterday and less than tomorrow."
- Rosemonde Gérard

"Wild nights - Wild nights!
Were I with thee
Wild nights should be
Our luxury!"
- Emily Dickinson

"Every heart sings a song, incomplete,
until another heart whispers back. Those who wish
to sing always find a song. At the touch of love,
everyone becomes a poet."
- Plato

"Adieu, dear heart, nothing but death
can make me cease to love you."
- Marie Antoinette

"…love, the breaking of your soul upon my lips."
- E. E. Cummings

"There is no charm equal to tenderness
of the heart."
- Jane Austen

"A woman knows the face of the man she loves
as a sailor knows the open sea."
- Honoré de Balzac

"And ever has it been known that love knows not
its own depth until the hour of separation."
- Khalil Gibran

"Sake shows true feelings."
- Japanese Proverb

"Even in my dreams, I never imagined that I should
find so much love on earth."
- Prince Albert (to Queen Victoria)

"Love, like rain, does not choose the grass
on which it falls."
- African Proverb

"Your words are my food; your breath, my wine.
You are everything to me."
- Sarah Bernhardt

Sir Walter Raleigh, said to have written on a
window with a diamond to Queen Elizabeth I:
"Fain would I climb, but yet fear I to fall."

Queen Elizabeth I: "If thy heart fails thee,
then climb not at all."

"Hear my soul speak. Of the very instant that I saw you, did my heart fly to your service."
- *William Shakespeare*

"I have seen only you, I have admired only you, I desire only you."
- *Napoleon Bonaparte*

"She blushed, and so did he. She greeted him in a faltering voice, and he spoke to her without knowing what he was saying."
- *Candide*, Voltaire

"Love is never lost. If not reciprocated, it will flow back and soften and purify the heart."
- *Washington Irving*

"It is a curious thought, but it is only when
you see people looking ridiculous, that you
realize just how much you love them."
- Agatha Christie

"Nothing in the world is single;
All things by law divine
In one spirit meet and mingle.
Why not I with thine?"
- Percy Bysshe Shelley

"Whatever souls are made of,
his and mine are the same."
- Emily Brontë

"Nobody has ever measured, not even poets,
how much the heart can hold."
- Zelda Fitzgerald

"It is better to have loved and lost,
than to have never loved at all."
- Alfred, Lord Tennyson

"Come live with me and be my love…"
- Christopher Marlowe

"Seduce me. Write letters to me.
And poems, I love poems. Ravish me
with your words. Seduce me."
- Anne Boleyn

"How do I love thee? Let me count the ways.
I love thee to the depth and breadth
and height my soul can reach…."
- Elizabeth Barrett Browning

"…but for those who love, time is eternity."
- Henry Van Dyke

"Always look your best – who said love is blind?"
- Mae West

"Love is blind."
- Geoffrey Chaucer

la douleur exquise:
(n.) the heart-wrenching pain of wanting
the affection of someone unattainable

"If you want to be loved, be loveable."
- Ovid

"Every once in a while, right in the middle of
an ordinary life, love gives us a fairytale."
- Anonymous

"I retain an unalterable affection for you, which
neither time or distance can change."
- George Washington

"Love Jo all your days, if you choose,
but don't let it spoil you, for it's wicked
to throw away so many good gifts
because you can't have the one you want."
- Little Women, Louisa May Alcott

"Never love anyone who treats you
like you're ordinary."
- Oscar Wilde

"…for me there lies, within the lights and shadows
of your eyes, the only beauty
that is never old."
- James Weldon Johnson

"I am sorry I can say nothing more consoling
to you, for love in action is a harsh and dreadful
thing compared to love in dreams."
- Fyodor Dostoevsky

"The course of true love never did run smooth."
- William Shakespeare

"Don't try to make someone hate the person
he loves, for he will go on loving,
but he will hate you."
- African Proverb

"Love is when he gives you a piece of your soul that you never knew was missing."

- Torquato Tasso

"When you love, you should not think you can direct the course of love, for love, if it finds you worthy, directs your course."

- Khalil Gibran

"Being deeply loved by someone gives you strength, while loving someone deeply gives you courage."

- Lao Tzu

"Love is a condition in which the happiness of another person is essential to your own."

- Robert A. Heinlein

"Love sought is good, but given unsought,
is better."
- William Shakespeare

"One's first love is always perfect,
until one meets one's second love."
- Elizabeth Aston

"A mighty pain to love it is,
And 't is a pain that pain to miss;
But of all pains, the greatest pain
It is to love, but love in vain."
- Abraham Cowley

"My love is selfish.
I cannot breathe without you."
- John Keats

"You know it's love when all you want is that person to be happy, even if you're not part of their happiness."

- Julia Roberts

"The sweetest joy, the wildest woe is love."

- Philip James Bailey

"I love you. These three words have my life in them."

- Alix of Hesse

"True love never has a happy ending because true love never ends."

- Alexander the Great

"If you love everything, you will perceive the divine mystery in things. Once you have perceived it, you will begin to comprehend it better every day, and you will come at last to love the world with an all-embracing love."

- *Fyodor Dostoevsky*

"I think... if it is true that there are as many minds as there are heads, then there are as many kinds of love as there are hearts."

- Leo Tolstoy

"There is no limit to the power of loving."

- John Morton

"The greatest happiness in life is the conviction that we are loved; loved for ourselves, or rather, loved in spite of ourselves."

- Victor Hugo

"I have no notion of loving people by halves; it is not in my nature."

- Jane Austen

"Let us always meet each other with a smile,
for a smile is the beginning of love."

- Mother Teresa

"Years of love have been forgot in the
hatred of a minute."

- Edgar Allan Poe

"Love one another and help others to rise
to the higher levels simply by pouring out love.
Love is infectious and the greatest
healing energy."

- Sai Baba of Shirdi

"There is only one happiness in life:
to love and be loved."

- George Sand

41

"You, yourself, as much as anybody in the entire
universe, deserves your love and affection."

- Sharon Salzberg

"The greatest degree of inner tranquility
comes from the development of love
and compassion. The more we care for
the happiness of others, the greater
is our own sense of well-being."

- Dalai Lama

"Love and you shall be loved."

- Ralph Waldo Emmerson

"Fall in love with yourself, then life, then with
whoever you want."

- Frida Kahlo

"Every kind of love is love, but self-love
is supreme among them."
- African Proverb

"Love yourself first and everything else falls in line.
You really have to love yourself to get anything
done in this world."
- Lucille Ball

"Not all of us can do great things,
but we can do small things
with great love."
- Mother Teresa

"We are shaped and fashioned
by what we love."
- Johann Wolfgang von Goethe

"For true love is inexhaustible; the more you give
the more you have."
- Antoine de Saint-Exupery

"There is nothing truly more artistic
than to love people."
- Vincent Van Gogh

"Wherever you have friends, that's your country.
Wherever you have love,
that's your home."
- Tibetan Proverb

"The love you give away is the only
love you keep."
- Elbert Hubbard

"Nothing can be accomplished without love."
- Henry Matisse

"No one is born hating another person
because of the color of his skin, or his background,
or his religion. People must learn to hate, and
if they can learn to hate, they can be taught to love,
for love comes more naturally to the human
heart than its opposite."
- Nelson Mandela

"Wherever you are and whatever you do,
be in love."
- Rumi

"Don't forget to love yourself."
- Soren Kierkegaard

"Instinctively, men feel the love clothed
in whatever language."
- Swami Vivekananda

"When you put love out in the world it travels, and
it can touch people and reach people in ways that
we never even expected."
- Laverne Cox

"If you don't love yourself, nobody will. Not only
that, you won't be good at loving anyone else.
Loving starts with the self."
- Wayne Dyer

"How you love yourself is how you teach
others to love you."
- Rupi Kaur

"If you have only one smile in you, give it
to the people you love."
- *Maya Angelou*

"There is no remedy for love but to love more."
- *Henry David Thoreau*

"When we love, we always strive to become
better than we are. When we strive to become
better than we are, everything around us
becomes better, too."
- *Paulo Coelho*

"Sometimes it's a form of love just to talk to
somebody that you have nothing in common with
and still be fascinated by their presence."
- *David Byrne*

"Love is to understand, at last,
the suffering of another."
- Pam Brown

"If you have love in your life, it can make
up for a great many things that are missing.
If you don't have love in your life, no matter
what else there is, it's not enough."
- Ann Landers

"When the power of love overcomes the love
of power, the world will know peace."
- Jimi Hendrix

"When you love what you have,
you have everything you need."
- Unknown

"The best portion of a man's life:
his little, nameless, unremembered acts
of kindness and love."
- William Wordsworth

"Speak with love and it becomes truth."
- Sai Baba of Shirdi

"We can cure physical diseases with medicine,
but the only cure for loneliness, despair,
and hopelessness is love. There are many in the
world who are dying for a piece of bread but there
are many more dying for a little love."
- Mother Teresa

"And now these three remain:
faith, hope, and love. But the greatest
of these is love."

- 1 Corinthians 13:13

love   pag-ibig   amare   salang
aahkyit   liefde   kärlek   milovat
kærlighed   rakkaus   aimer   liebe
pyaar   updendo   soyayya   aloha
grá   armastus   ást   hak   szeretet
jacayl   asanninneq   cinta   laska
uthando   hlub   aroha   mohabbat
libe   evin   imhabba   yêu   meilė
alofa   prēma   miłość   ai   anpu
pi'āra   dragoste   khair   lyubov
gaol   tresna   dashuri   adaraya
sneha   ài   maitri   sevgi   cariad
agapi   maitasuna   rąk   hobb   aşk
renmen   ljubav   amore   mīlestība

ENDING THOUGHTS

While it would be impossible to find and include quotes representing all the ways we process and feel about love, I hope you enjoyed reading *Love: Heartfelt Quotes* as much as I enjoyed pouring through and compiling these many quotations.

More importantly, however, I hope you found meaning and perhaps some recollections of your own through these words – timeless snippets of thoughts, experiences, and observations about love through the centuries.

Please look for the next book in the series, *Joy*, coming soon in 2022.

With love and thanks,

Claire B.

SOURCES

"1 Corinthians 13:4–8." *Bible Gateway*, www.biblegateway.com
/passage/?search=1%20Corinthians%2013%3A4-
8&version=NIV. Accessed 27 July 2022.

"1 Corinthians 13:13." *Bible Gateway*, www.biblegateway.com/passage
/?search=1+Corinthians+13%3A13&version=NIV.
Accessed 27 July 2022.

"18 Interesting Quotes by Anne Boleyn." *The Famous People*, quotes
.thefamouspeople.com/anne-boleyn-727.php. Accessed 27
July 2022.

50 Jimi Hendrix Quotes. (2022, June 11). Upjourney. Retrieved August
28, 2022, from https://upjourney.com/jimi-hendrix-
quotes

"69 Insightful Alexander the Great Quotes." *The Famous People*,
quotes.thefamouspeople.com/alexander-the-great-653
.php. Accessed 29 July 2022.

"8 Top Marie Antoinette Quotes." *The Famous People*, quotes
.thefamouspeople.com/marie-antoinette-2257.php.
Accessed 28 July 2022.

"Abraham Cowley Quotes." *Love Expands Media*, loveexpands.com
/quotes/abraham-cowley-5998. Accessed 8 Aug. 2022.

"Agatha Christie Quote." *LibQuotes*, libquotes.com/agatha-christie
/quote/lbw1z0c. Accessed 2 Aug. 2022.

Almeida, Laura. "Quotes from Frida Kahlo." *Denver Art Museum*, 28
Dec. 2020, www.denverartmuseum.org/en/blog/quotes-
frida-kahlo.

Ansari, Nashrah. "40 Tibetan Proverbs." *Feeding Trends*, 30 Dec. 2020, feedingtrends.com/tibetan-proverbs-sayings-life-etiquette-knowledge-wisdom.

"As Is The Sea Marvelous." *Hello Poetry*, hellopoetry.com/poem/1556/as-is-the-sea-marvelous. Accessed 2 Aug. 2022.

"As Is The Sea Marvelous." *Hello Poetry*, hellopoetry.com/poem /1556/as-is-the-sea-marvelous. Accessed 2 Aug. 2022.

"Beautiful Romantic Quotes by John Keats." *Quotabulary.Com*, quotabulary.com/beautiful-romantic-quotes-by-john-keats. Accessed 28 July 2022.

"Beauty That Is Never Old." *Poets.Org*, Academy of American Poets, 7 June 2020, poets.org/poem/beauty-never-old.

Coffey, Sally. "Queen Victoria and Prince Albert: A Royal Love Story." *The Official Magazine Britain*, www.britain-magazine.com/features/royals/queen-victoria-and-prince-albert-a-royal-love-story. Accessed 2 Aug. 2022.

Coleman, Nia. "Top 10 Revolutionary Nelson Mandela Quotes on Love." *The Borgen Project*, 3 Sept. 2019, borgenproject.org /nelson-mandela-quotes-on-love.

Cornelius, Mackensie. "15 Chinese Proverbs About Love for the Romantic Learner." *FluentU*, 27 Feb. 2022, www.fluentu .com/blog/chinese/chinese-proverbs-about-love.

"Edgar Allen Poe." *Edgar Allan Poe Society of Baltimore*, 14 Jan. 2018, www.eapoe.org/works/poems/tome.htm.

Enany, Mariam. "How to Say I Love You in Arabic (Egyptian Dialect)." *Talk in Arabic*, talkinarabic.com/Egyptian /phrases/i-love-you/#:~:text=Love%20as%20a %20noun%20is,and%20second%20person%20feminine% 20respectively. Accessed 13 Sept. 2022.

Evans, Erin. "15 Beautiful Maya Angelou Love Quotes." *Bright Drops*, brightdrops.com/maya-angelou-love-quotes. Accessed 23 Aug. 2022.

"Fairy Quotes." *QuotesPictures.Com*, quotespictures.com/every-once-in-a-while-in-the-middle-of-an-ordinary-life-love-gives-us-a-fairytale. Accessed 2 Aug. 2022.

Fischel, Ben. "Fyodor Dostoevsky Quotes." *Project Monkey Mind*, 1 Mar. 2020, www.projectmonkeymind.com/ 2020/03/ dostoevsky-quotes.

"George Washington Quote." *Mount Vernon*, www.mountvernon.org /library/digitalhistory/quotes/article/i-retain-an-unalterable-affection-for-you-which-neither-time-or-distance-can-change. Accessed 28 July 2022.

Guillen, Carmen. "20 Literary Love Quotes." *Actualidad Literatura*, www.actualidadliteratura.com/en/las-20-mejores-citas-de-amor-de-la-literatura. Accessed 31 July 2022.

"Helen Keller Love Quotes." *Pure Love Quotes*, www.purelovequotes .com/author/helen-keller. Accessed 29 July 2022.

"Henri Matisse Quote." *Status Town*, statustown.com/quote/15416. Accessed 2 Aug. 2022.

"Henry Van Dyke Quotes." *Love Expands*, loveexpands.com/quotes /henry-van-dyke-326225. Accessed 2 Aug. 2022.

Houghton, Eve. "How Do I Love Thee? Let Me Count the Ways (Sonnets from the Portuguese 43)." *LitCharts*, 8 May 2019. Accessed 28 July 2022.

Jenkins, Cameron, and Larry Stansbury. "122 Best Love Quotes That Prove True Romance Really Does Exist." *Good Housekeeping*, 19 Aug. 2022, www.goodhousekeeping.com /life/relationships/g3721/quotes-about-love.

Juma, Norbert. "80 Dalai Lama Quotes on Life, Love and Compassion." *Everyday Power*, 29 June 2022, everydaypower.com/dalai-lama-quotes-on-life.

"Khalil Gibran Quote." *Minimalist Quotes*, minimalistquotes.com /khalil-gibran-quote-3330. Accessed 2 Aug. 2022.

Kubasak, John. "10 Of the Most Beautiful Mother Teresa Quotes On Love." *Mystical Humanity of Christ*, www.coraevans .com/blog/article/10-of-the-most-beautiful-mother-teresa-quotes-on-love. Accessed 31 July 2022.

Kremer, James. "Native American Proverbs I Love." *Medium.Com*, 2 Aug. 2020, medium.com/love-quotes-of-the-day/native-american-proverbs-i-love-6ceca0bbac7a.

"Love and You Shall Be Loved." *Quote Park*, quotepark.com/quotes /1311988-ralph-waldo-emerson-love-and-you-shall-be-loved. Accessed 2 Aug. 2022.

"Love In Different Languages." *App2Brain*, app2brain.com/learn-languages/words-phrases/love. Accessed 30 July 2022.

"Love Is Quotes." *Brainy Quote*, www.brainyquote.com/topics/love-is-quotes. Accessed 28 July 2022.

"Love Quotes." *Good Reads*, www.goodreads.com/quotes/tag/love? Accessed 27 July 2022.

"Love Quotes." *Love Quoter*, www.lovequoter.com/love_quotes. Accessed 28 July 2022.

"Love Will Win: 15 Love Quotes From Black History Makers." *Uneek*, 4 June 2020, www.uneekjewelry.com/blog/love-quotes-black-history-makers.

Memoryslandscape. "On A Night When the Moon Shines As Brightly As…" *Tumblr*, 11 January 2018, memoryslandscape.tumblr.com/post/169602736083/on-a-night-when-the-moon-shines-as-brightly-as

"Napoleon Bonaparte Love Quotes and Sayings." *Love Quotes and Sayings*, 31 July 2022, lovequotes.symphonyoflove.net /napoleon-bonaparte-love-quotes-and-love-sayings.html.

Nelson, Kristin. "Wild nights - Wild nights!." LitCharts. LitCharts LLC, 7 Jan 2020. Accessed 30 Jul 2022.

"Nicholas and Alexandra, A Romanov Romance." *A La Vieille Russie*, www.alvr.com/4276/alvr-blog-nicholas-alexandra-a-romanov-romance. Accessed 1 Aug. 2022.

Owens, Alexandra. "30 Of Our Favorite Quotes About Love." *Town & Country*, 27 Jan. 2022, www.townandcountrymag.com/ leisure/arts-and-culture/tips/g522/best-love-quotes.

Pam Brown Quotes. (n.d.). Picture Quotes. Retrieved August 28, 2022, from http://www.picturequotes.com/pam-brown-quotes

Pannell, Ni'Kesia. "120 Romantic Love Quotes To Show Someone Special How Much They Mean To You." *Woman's Day*, 9 Feb. 2022, www.womansday.com/relationships /a38346873/quotes-about-love/#.

"Percy Bysshe Shelley Quote." *Quote Catalog*, quotecatalog.com/quote/percy-bysshe-shelley-nothing-in-the-Z7240Aa. Accessed 2 Aug. 2022.

Phillips, Lauren. "40 Love Quotes to Help You Express How You Feel." *Real Simple*, 7 Jan. 2022, www.realsimple.com/work-life/family/relationships/love-quotes.

"Philosopher Love Quotes." *No Sweat Shakespeare*, nosweatshakespeare.com/quotes/literature/love-quotes-philosophers. Accessed 27 July 2022.

"Queen Elizabeth I Quotes." *Good Reads*, www.goodreads.com /author/quotes/4380234.Elizabeth_I?page=2. Accessed 27 July 2022. `

"Quotes for: Love." *Bubo Quote*, www.buboquote.com/en/quotes/tag/2-love. Accessed 30 July 2022.

"Quotes About Love." *Art Quotes*, www.art-quotes.com/getquotes.php?catid=180#.YucqynbMIVA. Accessed 29 July 2022.

"Rabindranath Tagore Love Quotes." *Pure Love Quotes*, www.purelovequotes.com/author/rabindranath-tagore. Accessed 31 July 2022.

"Rosemonde Gerard Quotes." *Good Reads*, www.goodreads.com/quotes/243073-for-you-see-each-day-i-love-you-more-today. Accessed 27 July 2022.

Sacasas, Caitlin. "47 Japanese Proverbs About Life, Love, and Wisdom to Inspire You." *Fluent in 3 Months*, www.fluentin3months.com/japanese-proverbs. Accessed 29 July 2022.

"Sai Baba Quotes." *Brainy Quote*, www.brainyquote.com/authors/sai-baba-quotes. Accessed 30 July 2022.

Scanlan, James. "How to Say Love in 50 Languages With Europe in a Day!" *Europe in a Day*, 2021, europeinaday.wordpress.com/2021/02/03/how-to-say-love-in-50-languages-with-europe-in-a-day

Schiffman, Richard. "Ancient India's 5 Words for Love (And Why Knowing Them Can Heighten Your Happiness)." *Yes! Solutions Journalism*, 14 Aug. 2014, www.yesmagazine.org/health-happiness/2014/08/14/ancient-india-s-five-words-for-love.

"Shakespeare Love Quotes." *No Sweat Shakespeare*, nosweatshakespeare.com/quotes/categories/love Accessed 27 July 2022.

Sharpe, Rachel. "150+ Love Quotes to Increase Your Self Esteem." *Declutter the Mind*, 23 Dec. 2021, declutterthemind.com/blog/self-love-quotes.

"She Walks in Beauty." *Poetry Foundation*, www.poetryfoundation.org
/poems/43844/she-walks-in-beauty. Accessed 28 July
2022.

"Shutterfly Community. "120+ I Love You Quotes: Famous Love
Quotes for All." *Shutterfly*, 22 July 2022, www.shutterfly
.com/ideas/i-love-you-quotes

Song to Celia (Drink To Me With Thine Eyes)." *Poetry Foundation*,
www.poetryfoundation.org/poems/44464/song-to-celia-
drink-to-me-only-with-thine-eyes. Accessed 27 July 2022.

"Swami Vivekananda's Quotes on Love." *VivekaVani*, 15 Mar. 2019,
vivekavani.com/swami-vivekananda-quotes-love.

The Editors. "66 Buddha Quotes." *Up Journey*, 20 Oct. 2019,
upjourney.com/buddha-quotes.

"Top 6 Quotes of Emilie Loring." *Inspiring Quotes*,
www.inspiringquotes.us/author/5771-emilie-loring.
Accessed 29 July 2022.

"Unrequited Love Picture Quotes Tumblr." *Relatably.Com*,
relatably.com/q/unrequited-love-picture-quotes-tumblr.
Accessed 31 Aug. 2022.

Tripathy, Anwesha. "30 Famous Quotes From Indian Personalities
About Love and Kindness." *ScrollDroll*, 3 Nov. 2021,
**www.scrolldroll.com/famous-quotes-from-indian-
personalities.**

Voltaire Quotes." *Inspirational Stories*, www.inspirationalstories.com
/quotes/voltaire-she-blushed-and-so-did-he-she-greeted.
Accessed 1 Aug. 2022.

"Wolfgang Amadeus Quotes and Sayings." *Inspiring Quotes*,
www.inspiringquotes.us/author/7540-wolfgang-amadeus-
mozart. Accessed 28 July 2022.

Zulu, Samuel. "60 African Proverbs About Love (In Its Purest Form)." *Trials and Tests*, 31 Jan. 2020, trialsandtests.com /60-african-proverbs-about-love-in-its-purest-form.

www.ingramcontent.com/pod-product-compliance
Lightning Source LLC
Chambersburg PA
CBHW051647120626
46551CB00015B/2248